Servant Leadership Roadmap

Master the 12 Core Competencies of Management
Success with Leadership Qualities and Interpersonal
Skills

Cara Bramlett

Clinical Minds Leadership Development Series, Book 2

Disclaimer and FTC Notice

I may use affiliate links and affiliate products I have used and found useful in the contents. If you decide to make a purchase, I will get a sales commission. This does not reflect that my opinion is for sale. I encourage you to do your own research before making any purchase online.

ISBN-13: 978-1982058685

ISBN-10: 1982058684

Table of Contents

Hi there!

Congratulations! You are committed to your development and understanding skills to become the most effective leader possible!

I'm so excited to meet you and guide you on this leadership journey!

Do you wish you knew . . .

- How some managers lead rock-star teams and always deliver above expectations?
- How some managers have unwavering devotion of their team members?
- How some individuals can command a room and have others follow them?
- Why your team doesn't give you a heads-up of known failures or challenges?

I am going to share these answers with you!

If you are a leader thriving to drive leadership excellence, brush up on competencies, and refresh your skills, this is the perfect place.

You will find this book full of useful content without fluff. You will be able to immediately institute your refreshed skills into your daily leadership.

Leadership begins with having the right skills onboard and tools in your mental toolbox to guide you to success.

This book is chock-full of real-life examples, a few medical analogies, and tons of helpful techniques. You will also discover lots of helpful templates and guides for coaching, decision making, task delegation, and more!

Download the toolbox by checking out the link below!

www.facebook.com/carabramlett/

You will discover your personal leadership style, personal listening style, and a way to develop your current team into a high performing group of individuals.

The foundation of this book is through servant leadership. We lead individuals through emotional connections, trust, and inspiration.

Click below to receive your **FREE** bonus material!

The keys to **UNLOCK** your management **SUCCESS**!

www.facebook.com/carabramlett/

Servant leadership is best represented by the paradoxes of being a servant-leader in the poem below:

Strong enough to be weak
Successful enough to fail
Busy enough to make time
Wise enough to say "I don't know"
Serious enough to laugh
Rich enough to be poor
Right enough to say "I'm wrong"
Compassionate enough to discipline
Mature enough to be childlike
Important enough to be last
Planned enough to be spontaneous
Controlled enough to be flexible
Free enough to endure captivity
Knowledgeable enough to ask questions
Loving enough to be angry
Great enough to be anonymous

Responsible enough to play
Assured enough to be rejected
Victorious enough to lose
Industrious enough to relax
Leading enough to serve

Poem by Brewer, as cited by Hansel, in Holy Sweat,
Dallas Texas, Word, 1987. (p. 29)

This journey will not be easy. However, it is filled with rewards. Lastly, I will empower you with tools to further your leadership and identify the areas to strengthen your leadership success.

I'm excited about our journey! Let's get started!

Cara Bramlett

Leadership Excellence

Competency goes beyond words. It's the leader's ability to say it, plan it, and do it in such a way that others know that you know how—and know that they want to follow you.

—John C. Maxwell

You feverishly shuffle the papers on your desk, mentally scrambling for reasons as to why you blatantly missed the goal and key objectives. You subconsciously scan through the disorganized reports, searching for any nugget that could provide a gleam of hope. Your mind is bouncing from one employee to another.

How could they do this to me? Again?

Why are they not following my simple instructions?

You mentally analyze their performance over the past several months: *Why am I the manager with the worst employees? I would rather have other employees as names.* Faces flood your mind.

The shrill buzz of your phone intercom system jars you from your inner confessions. Your manager is ready for your update.

Oh, no! It's time! Your stomach becomes queasy and you swallow hard.

You nervously walk down the long hallway, giving yourself a pep talk and mentally rehearsing rebuttals to execute over the next painstaking hour.

Reaching the door, you close your eyes and take a deep breath. Your fingers grip the cold metal doorknob, and the door slightly creaks as it opens. You enter, attempting to maintain your composure as your thoughts race and your heart pounds in your throat.

Your manager looks up with a blank, emotionless stare. His bifocals are meticulously resting on the tip off his square nose. His brows are furrowed and forearms propped on the edge of his desk. His noteworthy gold pen is held steady in his right hand.

You take a deep breath and begin rapidly explaining the challenges faced, failed technology. and inexperience of your team. The difficulty of working with others within the organization. Their lack of response that impedes your ability to meet the goal.

Yes! This is it! He is understanding! Good job!

Nope!

Your manager holds up his right hand with the gold pen glistening. He lowers his head. You know that it's the nonverbal cue to stop. He asks you to sit down and just listen.

You slump down in the chair, defeated, knowing you have disappointed him once again.

It's not my fault! It's my employees! How can he not understand? Doesn't he remember I'm still new at this management job?

He places the gold pen on the stack of papers and leans back in his chair, looking at you with stoic brown eyes. He begins to speak in soft, deep tone that you have never heard.

He shares the secrets of leadership success and the guaranteed ability to influence individuals you don't directly manage. We are guided by our moral compass. Our inner sense that directs us to act with integrity and ethical behavior.

It becomes evident that he is devoted to your development and divulging these ironclad leadership principles. He shares authentic leadership begins with treating your employees as partners. You must develop your interpersonal skills and leadership qualities to achieve management success.

You must know yourself and your core values.

Understand that you need your team more than they need you. Without authentic leadership, you will turn around and have no one to lead. Create a culture of trust, be humble, and inspire others.

All leaders have moments of weakness and find themselves straying from their core principles. We start to blame others for failures and not accept responsibility. We stop holding ourselves to the same standards as our team. It is human nature and why leaders are learners. We are always developing.

Picking up the gold pen, he shares that it all begins with developing your core competencies.

Competencies are the attributes to complete a specific job. Competencies consist of skills, knowledge, and abilities. These attributes define a set of characteristics that are create value within the organization to meet the values, mission, and vision. Each position will have defined competencies to successfully complete the job. Cultural fit will determine if you are suitable to the culture of the specific organization.

Leadership excellence thrives on the continued development of key leadership-derived competencies. Each one unique to situations that could be encountered along your journey. Understanding and knowing how to leverage each skill will ensure your success in your path. Embrace the competencies and develop your skills to know how to best apply the new knowledge.

As an individual, there are many resources available today to provide insight of your current leadership skills and your leadership development opportunities. Resources could include self-assessments through the more popular strength-based design, personality type, or 360 self-assessments, to name a few. Your human resources representative or company-based learning tools are resources that could be helpful along your journey.

By understanding the deficits in your management style, a custom professional development agenda can be created and further tailored to your current leadership position. I will show you how to leverage your resources to be stewards of your own professional development.

Taking time to understand your management deficits will demonstrate growth. Developing your deficits will yield excellence in your position.

How does that sound?

The most critical quality of any leader is understanding the importance of the team. Without a team, you will have no one to lead. Leadership is the ability to inspire someone. This requires a deep understanding of the team members and each member's aspirations.

What are the individual's goals? What are the

motivations? Have you taken time to ask them? If not, you are falling short. How can you inspire or motivate your team without knowing who they are?

You need your team more than they need you.

Leaders are compensated for the performance of our team—good or bad. If the team fails, we fail as their leader. Our job as leaders is to remove barriers and roadblocks to secure the team's success. The team's success is our measuring stick. Consider the obstacles that are creating difficulty for the team. Identify solutions for the obstacles and how to remove them.

Many managers begin their careers with I'm-the-boss-so-do-as-I-say mentality. Most leaders start with this approach, which is understandable. You will soon learn that this autocratic style of leadership will impact your ability to lead and have influential leadership effectively.

Be sincere and honest in your inspiration to team members; listen, inquire about them, and speak less about yourself. Leverage your emotional intelligence to understand their positions and manage your personal emotions.

Maintaining transparency and honesty are key to gaining an individual's trust. One of the most missed opportunities as a leader is not admitting mistakes. Honesty is demonstrated through admitting one's faults. Although all leaders want to succeed, but part of being a great leader is taking risks and be willing to fail. Attempting failure as well as success is important. Admitting when something didn't go as planned is part of what will demonstrate honesty to the team.

Demonstrating honesty and achieving trust will increase your ability to have influential leadership. Don't play the blame game and just own mistakes. The mistake will also provide the opportunity of how to manage through failure. creating an action plan of how to respond to the mistake, and find success in the failure.

In the following chapters, you will learn that mastering leadership competencies are vital to the success of any leadership role. Leaders leverage the power of influence to achieve outcomes. Leaders empower individuals and remove barriers. Leaders demonstrate strong will, acceptance of responsibility, and develop skills.

To lead a strong team and achieve leadership excellence, we must embrace a growth mindset. We start by thinking of our employees and organizational partners as team members. Our employees are our team members and not our subordinate. We are partners, first and foremost. Our goal is not to control another individual. Our goal as leaders is to lead, inspire, and guide others by influence. Influence begins by understanding our leadership style and our team members.

Leadership Styles

The best leaders don't know just one style of leadership; they're skilled at several and have the flexibility to switch between styles as the circumstance dictate.

—Daniel Goleman

Do you know your style?

To truly understand the essence of servant leadership, one must understand the different types of leadership. The leader must evaluate oneself to recognize what kind of leadership style he or she naturally exhibits. This will help in making a clearer judgment towards guiding the team.

Individuals can sense when a leader is disingenuous to representing oneself. Be genuine and consistent in leading the team. Acting on an unnatural style will leave an impression of uncertainty and question your credibility to lead.

Each leadership style is unique, and based upon the presenting situation, you will leverage one style over another. The foundation of leadership will guide you on the best style to use. There is no magic combination for success. Each situation is analyzed for the best approach.

In 1930, Lewin defined three psychology-based leadership styles: autocratic, democratic, and laissez-faire. These styles are still commonly used today as leadership style descriptions.

Autocratic style demands immediate compliance. As the word denotes, this is the do-as-you-are-told kind of leader. This kind of leadership style can be advised in situations that warrant an immediate action. However, when used continuously, it will result in discontent among the team. This style is effective to get people from a burning building or out of gunfire. It is effective during a code or in the critical care unit when someone goes into cardiac arrest. It is not beneficial when modifying the behavior of our team and often met with resistance. Be cautious when using it.

Democratic style is consensus through participation. The democratic leader is one who builds trust and achieves goals through voting, consensus, or collaboration. This kind of leader tends to ask questions and reaches agreements. Consider this style when you are rolling out a new process or initiative. Develop a small focus group to define the process, expectations, workflow, etc.

There will always be elements you do not consider because you are not doing the job every day. Bring in your subject matter experts (i.e., team members) and collaborate. This will also provide an avenue for the team's buy-in.

Laissez-faire style is based on the mindset of building a strong team and staying out of their way. It is the opposite of autocratic leadership. Here the individuals are given loosely defined objectives and goals. One of the most significant benefits of this style is innovation. This style can be frustrating to individuals who want clearly defined objectives.

In 1964, business-minded professionals Robert Blake and Jane Mouton focused on two styles: task-oriented and people-oriented.

Task-oriented style is focused on results-driven outcomes. In this style, the leader ensures clear communication and expectations of the objectives and desired outcomes. The consideration of who is most appropriate for the task is not considered.

People-oriented style is focused on determining which team member is most suited for a task based upon his or her current skill set, interest, or personal development. This style is effective for developing an individual through stretch opportunities. Stretch opportunities are tasks given to individuals that are above his or her skill set and intended to push the individual out of his or her comfort zone to promote development.

In 2002, Daniel Goleman detailed the six emotional styles of leadership including visionary, coaching, affiliate, democratic, pacesetting, and commanding.

Visionary style moves people towards a vision. This is said to be the most impactful style of leadership. This kind of leader gains strength through passion and vision. The coach empowers the individuals. This style empowers and inspires the team. It often drives innovation and creativity. Convey the vision and get out of the team's way.

Coaching style develops people for the future. This is a kind of leader whose focus is on achieving progress. Every single person on your team needs coaching in some capacity. The individual's goal may not be a management path. Focusing on the individual's goal could be as simple as demonstrating excellence in my everyday job or enhancing my knowledge of treating diabetes.

Affiliate style creates emotional bonds. This is the people-come-first kind of leader in the sense that he or she tries as much as possible to build a bond or relationship. It is most effective in the phase of motivation when there's lack thereof among the team. This style is important to leverage when speaking with senior leaders. You represent the team and the team has chosen you. Keep this in mind and be mindful of how new initiatives will impact the team.

Pacesetter style expects excellence and self-direction. This is the kind of leader who is prone to set high standards without considering other's ideas. When used, it may damage their morale and make them feel inferior.

Pacesetting is appropriate when establishing a standard of care. For example, we consider our diabetic patients to be in control of the disease when the A1C is less than or equal to 7 percent. Leveraging pacesetting to drive productivity is not effective. Our goal as clinical professionals is to improve disease control of our patients. Improving disease control reduces the risk of complications. For diabetes, complications include blindness, dialysis, and limb amputation. Having this high standard is critical for this specific team.

Democratic style has previously been discussed and again focuses on consensus through participation.

The commanding style is equivalent to the do-as-you-are-told autocratic style of leadership as previously mentioned.

There are four additional styles of leadership defined and more of today's focus on leadership.

Transactional leadership is focused on the day-to-day operations. This leader has challenges with seeing the big picture or conveying a vision. Transactional leaders keenly focus on an individual's roles and responsibilities. They aggressively performance-manage team members who are not meeting expectations, thus leading to low morale.

Transformational leadership is a venue for innovation within an organization through inspiration and motivation of the team. These leaders are focused on transforming their organizations to the next level by leading with high-performing and engaged teams. This leadership is achieved through clear communication, conveying vision, integrity, emotional intelligence, authenticity, and self-awareness. This is the most common style in business.

Charismatic leadership encompasses the components of transformational leadership by inspiration and motivation. However, it is for the benefit of the leader. This leader is not focused on the innovation or excelling the organization. This style often leads to the demise of many organizations.

Servant leadership was first defined in 1970 by Robert Greenleaf as the natural desire to lead by serving others—meeting the needs of the team members, empowering them to make decisions, focus on growth, and ensures their basic needs are met.

Servant Leadership Roadmap

Many times, the servant-leader has no formal recognition. The leader is many times unknown and focuses the spotlight on the individual team members to show success.

The benefits of servant leadership are higher engagement, which leads to the high performance of the team. The team members feel valued and have a greater sense of engagement. They feel the leader cares about them and their well-being.

The team demonstrates high morale through guidance by a moral compass. This leader leads with high integrity, focuses on the good of the organization as well as the team members, is concerned with stakeholders, and exhibits a high degree of self-awareness.

There are the fundamental competencies of servant leadership that transcends all styles of leadership. Throughout the remainder of this book, you will learn these principles and when to apply them.

To be effective in leadership, one must know which style to leverage. Understanding that each style is critical depending on the situation and the environment you lead.

Now it's time to look in the mirror at yourself and enhance your self-awareness.

Competency 1: Self-Awareness

Self-awareness doesn't prevent you from making mistakes.

It allows you to learn from them.

—Anonymous

Self-awareness represents the ability to know yourself. Consider your passion, strengths, weaknesses, and emotions. What are your triggers? How do you emotionally respond to certain situations? Having a high level of self-awareness leads to the ability to represent your true self and know how your emotions affects your team. Self-awareness is demonstrated through confidence, being receptive of feedback, and honesty.

As a leader, you are always on stage, whether you notice it or not. Your team analyzes your actions, your mannerisms, words, and movement. Does your body language match your words? Self-regulation is the ability to manage your emotions during biological impulses. It's the emotional response to situations that arise.

Consider how you would respond to advising a patient of a devastating diagnosis such as cancer. You are strong, supportive, and optimistic. You advise the patient that there are options, and together you will overcome cancer.

Now consider the opposite. You advise the patient of a devastating diagnosis and break down in an emotional wreck. Your confused and distraught patient gives up and progresses in the illness.

As a leader, you must channel this same confident energy. Consider the situation, take a deep breath, and lead the team. Your team is looking for the same direction, strength, and hope as your patients. Our actions during tough times are what defines us as a leader.

Leveraging diversity

Being the leader does not mean you are required to know everything about every aspect you are leading. You were chosen for your position because someone identified leadership qualities in you. Recognize it. Embrace it. Build on it.

You cannot be an expert in every field you

manage. Attempting to do so will drive you nuts. You may even fail. Something or someone you lead will always fall short. Instead, surround yourself with subject matter experts in their discipline. By surrounding yourself with experts, you will ensure that you can be successful in any discipline.

Your instinct is to surround yourself with people who are similar to you. We must keep this in mind as leaders. We are drawn to individuals who share our likes and dislikes. Keep in mind that we are forming a team of experts to support a mission, not creating a new set of friends. Creating a team of like-minded individuals will ensure that you are surrounding yourself with individuals who share your strengths as well as your weaknesses.

It is critical to open doors to individuals who are not like you and whose strengths are your weakness. Opening doors will ensure a more well-rounded, high-functioning team. Individuals who challenge our thinking and provide different perspectives can be perceived as scary. As leaders, we must learn to embrace different opinions. Recognize this challenge as a good conflict, which will stimulate the growth of the team and individuals.

Delegation is empowerment

One of the greatest challenges as a leader is switching from doing to leading. You are empowerring someone else to do the tasks that don't require our unique skills. Personally, many leaders have a fear of becoming invisible and their staff receiving all the credit. Your team receiving credit for a job well done is a hidden jewel.

To other leaders, it demonstrates your ability to lead a high performing team. Recognize your team for their success personally and to the organization. The team member will develop a newfound loyalty to you, and you will be recognized for leading a strong team.

Another fear is losing control. The delegation of a task to another member of the team can feel like losing control of the task or the project. You are trusting that someone will do the task to the same standard that you perform. A chief nursing officer provided a great piece of advice early in my career: trust but verify. Yes, of course! Trust that the individuals will do the job to the same standard, and verify that they do! These three little words are powerful.

Ask yourself if your initiatives would advance if you were out of the office. If not, you are too involved and not empowering individuals to lead the charge. Understand why you are not delegating more initiatives. What are the barriers? What do you need to be successful? Tackle each of these instances.

One barrier could entail time restraint. It does require some time to identify the tasks completed and determine who would be best suited for the task. Also, you must factor in training the individual. Consider this as mentoring or developing the team member. Start thinking of delegation as growth of the individual team member and less of a burden on you.

When considering tasks to delegate, you should also consider tasks that aren't appropriate to delegate. Tasks that have unclear objectives, high stakes, rely on your unique skills, or a personal growth opportunity should be completed by you. Once you identify the tasks, it is easier to identify the person.

Now, we recognize delegation as growth opportunities for our team. We must also consider the skill sets for the tasks. Take a moment to identify the skills and competencies needed. Consider the individual and assess based on the following: skills, strengths, reliability, workload, and development potential.

As the tasks are delegated, keep the individuals' skills in mind. This will be a new endeavor for them and require you to build their self-confidence. This is why strength-and-skills matching is important. Set clear goals and routine check-ins. Also provide good feedback to the individuals on the progress. By doing so, you demonstrate a clear belief in the individual and their ability to perform the task.

It is very frustrating for team members to have a task and not have routine follow- up to ensure that they are meeting expectations.

In delegation and managing the task, set up an internal process. Note the defined objectives, goals, and deadline. Empower the individuals with needed resources and authority. Schedule routine check-ins and milestones. Most importantly, give credit where credit is due. Recognize the individuals for the work.

❖ Self-awareness recap:

Know yourself. The power of your leadership lies in knowing your strengths. We must surround ourselves with individuals different from us to compensate for our weaknesses. Leverage diversity in others to form a more well-rounded team.

View delegation as empowering and developing your team. Know your team and who is best suited for each task. Know yourself and your personal bias of delegation. Lastly, exercise self-awareness of your industry and concepts. Have a fundamental understanding to support your quality decisions.

Understanding self-awareness is the first step in achieving stewardship. We must know ourselves and our biases to be successful in stewardship. In the next chapter, we will learn how stewardship is accepting responsibility and accountability for our team as well as our own actions.

Competency 2: Stewardship

Management is doing the things right; leadership is doing the right things.

—*Peter F. Drucker*

Stewardship is demonstrated by taking responsibility and accountability. The leader's role is to be accountable to the members of the team through leading by example and removing barriers. Accountability is accepting the outcomes of an initiative, good or bad.

As servant-leaders, we must take responsibility for ourselves and the actions and performance of the team.

You need your team more than it needs you.

As leaders, we are compensated for the performance of our team—good or bad. If the team fails, we fail.

Our job as leaders is to remove barriers and roadblocks to secure the team's success. The team's success is our measuring stick. Consider the obstacles that are creating difficulty for the team. Identify solutions for the obstacles and how to remove them.

So how do we practice stewardship? It begins with leading by example.

Leading by example

To lead by example, we must be responsible for our actions. We must set the example for others to follow. Then we must follow the same rules, policies, and regulations we have required of the team.

For example, the supervisor cannot like a post on social media and performance management a team member for the same activity. Also, on the implementation of a strict travel provision, the leader cannot stay at the swankiest hotel in the city or initiate strict spending and purchase a luxury car.

Do any leaders immediately come to your mind? How does it make you feel? Aggravated? Angry? Frustrated?

If that statement stings, take a look in the mirror, think about your actions, and make changes.

Guess what? Your team feels the same way when you don't lead by example.

Servant Leadership Roadmap

Think before you act. All of our actions can impact our team. *Keep in mind that you are on stage and your team is watching.* The higher your position, the bigger your stage.

The do-as-I-say-and-not-as-I-do mentality is damaging to the morale of the team and damages your credibility as the leader. This double standard by the leader demoralizes the team and can become destructive. The team will feel a loss of the empathy and respect that you are trying to convey.

Think of your team as having a savings account. All of the trust, active listening, relationship building, etc. are small deposits into an account. Over time, you have a solid partnership and a nice nest egg with your team.

Each time you fail to lead by example causes a withdraw from the account. The amount of the withdrawal is determined by the actions of the leader. Betraying or perceived betrayal will result in large withdrawals leaving nothing in the account.

The result is you have lost the privilege to manage the team. Yes, leadership is a privilege.

It is an honor for a team to instill their trust in you to lead them. This privilege is not to be taken lightly. We are obligated to covet that trust by setting the best example and always having the team's best interest in mind.

Through leading by example, we demonstrate to

our team what is possible and begin practicing what we are preaching. Our teams begin thinking that our initiatives are possible to achieve because the leader is also doing them.

Leading by example is one of the secrets to getting team members to follow you. It is a small gesture that yields big returns and deposits into the team's virtual savings account. Over time, the team will follow you anywhere.

Leading by example can easily be applied to your leadership in several ways:

1. Be willing to do anything you would ask of others.

2. Follow the rules as closely as you expect your team members to follow.

3. Be cautious not to interrupt any team member, especially if you are critical of someone else interrupting.

4. If you allow the team to leave early, then you should also leave early. The team will feel guilty if you stay and finish the work.

Take a moment and think about your leadership style, your values, and your actions. Consider if you need to make any adjustments.

Next, let's focus on responsibility for actions of our team as well as yours.

Accepting responsibility

Good leaders take responsibility and bad leaders place blame.

Placing blame is often seen in leadership positions. When things go south, individuals are ready to point fingers and isolate the individual or thing that caused the issue. This is the easy route. It's much easier to point out someone and place blame.

Recognize that this is a detriment to everyone including the leadership you are attempting to establish. The blamed individual will feel betrayed by you, which will impact the trust you are developing as we will later learn. If we blame the process, the individual who created the process will feel betrayed.

What does placing blame represent? It signifies that the leader wasn't as prepared as one could have been. Think about that for a moment. When you point a finger at someone, there are three fingers pointing back at you.

Don't place blame; accept responsibility.

A responsible leader says, "I am the one who must make it happen." The leader will take the time to prepare and evaluates the needs of the team. This is demonstrated through several actions of the individual.

The leader takes responsibility for the actions—good or bad—of the team. We share the shortcomings of the team and have action plans in place to manage through obstacles. With any missed initiatives, blame is not placed.

In leading a team, leaders will relinquish the just-one-of-the-team position and rise to the leader position by setting direction and expectations for the group. This is shown by their separation from the team. You no longer go on lunches or friendly ventures outside of work. You rise to manage the problems and remove barriers. Leaders manage everyone with equality and integrity.

Stepping up and accepting responsibility can be viewed as an advantage. It is an opportunity for you to showcase our skills and abilities. If we accept blame, we then have a chance to show how we can manage in the face of adversity or through a crisis. This will advance your team, your initiatives, and your leadership reputation.

As you lead by example for accepting responsibility and accountability, you will see a change in the culture of your team. Your team members take ownership for outcomes. They also accept responsibility for their own actions and the job they perform. Collaboration is embraced and the team functions on a higher level.

Through stewardship, you have evolved your leadership and the team.

❖ Stewardship recap:

The stewardship competency is gained by leveraging our interpersonal skills of self-accountability and accepting responsibility. You hold yourself to the same standards and regulations of the team.

We accept responsibility for all actions—good or bad—of ourselves and those of our team. Achieve management success through developing solutions to obstacles and creating opportunities out of negative outcomes.

Competency 3: Motivation and Persuasion

Influence is the compass. Persuasion is the map.

Joseph Wong

Persuasion is a fundamental and essential proficiency of leadership. It is not by ill intention or manipulation. Consider persuasion as your ability to lead people in a specific direction on your behalf, regardless of your formal authoritative position.

Through persuasion, your leadership must appeal to a diverse group of individuals. You must make rational arguments and develop reasonable solutions.

To persuade your audience, you must first know your audience. Who is your audience? We convey a different message when addressing different classes or professions. Consider the occupation.

If I am persuading a clinical professional, I will focus the conservation on a medically related approach. With a mechanic or engineer, I will relate the topic to their unique occupational tasks. Know your audience and speak their language.

What's in it for me?

The number one message to communicate to an audience is the benefit of following the initiative you are conveying. The benefit must be tangible or something they can see or touch. What does the team get? Why should they follow? Think about the initiatives from all angles. Some benefits could include the following:

- Reduction in process steps
- Elimination of duplicate work
- Creating automated process to eliminate manual work
- Freeing up time for more desirable activities
- Improving safety records
- Status and recognition

These are just a few examples of potential benefits. There are millions of benefits. We must know our team members to know our best angle of persuasion. Knowing our team begins with knowing what motivates them.

Motivation represents the passion for the

drive. Motivation is demonstrated by the need to raise the bar and the status quo continuously. Your motivation to develop leadership is demonstrated today through reading this book. Individuals like you are viewed as having high work standards, goal-oriented, and committed to continuous professional development. Motivation is contagious. People naturally surround themselves with like-minded people. You are in good company.

To motivate your team for performance, you must understand your team and leverage the individual's engagement. Team engagement manifests by the team member's commitment to the organization's goals or values, the commitment to the success of the company, and the commitment to do their best every day. Each team member will have a different level of engagement, which may vary based on the current initiative.

Roughly, about 28 percent of disengaged team members leave a company, while only 4 percent are highly engaged. Many times, leaving is not financially driven. Consider the impact of having to replace an individual:

- increased workload
- downtime
- training for the new staff
- potential for fragmented care or failure to manage patients properly

- patients stop following treatment plans

Your opportunity is to leverage your leadership skills to drive engagement within your team.

We start by meeting the team members where they are and identifying the three levels of engagement:

Highly engaged: Think superstars—individuals who think about the job outside of working hours and don't consider the job "work." These individuals generally make your job easier. They are open to change and innovation. They are always working towards the end goal and looking for opportunities of growth.

Engaged: Think solid performers—individuals who consistently provide good work. Engaged individuals are essential for every team. These are the worker bees. These individuals are happy to do their jobs and do not desire additional responsibility. They are followers of the direction you set rather than active participants in evolving the model.

Disengaged: Think individuals who are not aligned with the position, team, mission, etc.—high-maintenance individuals, underperformers, etc. They can drag the team down. Many times, they require much of your attention and management.

These individuals can distract the team from the end goal, create chaos, and increase team drama. This instills uncertainty in your team.

Where does most of your team fall? Generally, 10 percent will be highly engaged, 80 percent engaged, and 10 percent disengaged.

To leverage engagement, you must know where you currently stand with your team. Ask for their honest feedback without reciprocity. It is vital to your growth as their leader. You will know where you need to adjust your shortcomings and focus on personal growth. Instill on the team the importance to provide you feedback as their leader. Reward the team for feedback. Keep in mind the partnership and growing together.

To engage the team, you must do so through a cultural change, not creating a program. Programs simply result in your superstars continuing to thrive as the unengaged continue with status quo. A motivated individual will work hard when there is something in it for them, while an engaged one will work hard for the sake of the company.

Every leader has the vision of creating a workplace that will draw in new team members due to the desirable environment.

What is the best technique to engage a group of individuals? The most effective technique I have discovered is described in Paul Marcino's *Carrots and Sticks Don't Work*. The RESPECT model is an acronym for the most effective aspects of engagement.

RESPECT represents recognition, empowerment, supportive feedback, partnership, expectations, consideration, and trust.

Recognition: Each team member desires to do a good job and be acknowledged for his or her commitment to the team. This will reinforce to the team the preferred behavior. Know your individual's preferred venue for recognition. Many, but not all, welcome being recognized in front of other team members, however. Individuals with underlying social anxiety will shy away and be embarrassed by public recognition. This could impede their future actions on goals. By knowing your team member, you will know their preferred venue of recognition.

Empowerment: Install in your team the trust to make decisions and function independently. You must support them through this avenue regardless of the decision made, and be mindful of micromanagement, ensuring that your team feels supported and will develop the confidence needed to make stronger decisions without questioning themselves. Delegate tasks that will showcase their unique skills.

Supportive feedback: Your job is to communicate feedback to the team to facilitate growth and the understanding of the goals and initiatives. Note that this feedback is supportive. The team members must receive the information as a personal growth opportunity, not a punitive one. Everyone is unique. You must identify the appropriate tone and structure of the conversation to instill the feedback without damaging the relationship.

Partnership: Leaders are partners with our team, not bosses. You are moving toward the same goal with slightly different jobs. You push each other to excel in your role and win as a team. You leverage transparency of ensuring the team is in the know of the current happenings.

Expectations are the defined goals that support the company's mission. As mentioned in the communication section, you must be clear in our expectations. The expectations should be clearly communicated and in writing to limit confusion of the team. You must also reinforce the expectations to keep the team on task and know the immediate prioritization. Vague expectations lead to underperforming teams and a poor reflection of your leadership.

Considerations: giving careful thought of how to interact with an individual. Leverage your emotional intelligence skills, and understand the position of each individual as it is rooted in his or her personality. Team members will feel you care for them and feel respected. Ask for the input of the individual doing the specific process before making changes that directly impact his or her daily activities. There is a high probability that they will provide you valuable feedback on how to gain efficiency. Make sure they know you have their best interest in mind and not checking up on them performing the job.

Trust is a common theme throughout this book, which should impress on you the value of trust of your team within your leadership role. This is the most pivotal element of any leader. It is the ability to make a good leader great and a mediocre leader fail.

Know where you currently stand with your team and ask for their feedback. It is vital to your growth as their leader. You will know where you need to adjust your shortcomings and focus on personal growth. Instill on the team the importance to provide you feedback as their leader, and stress the aspect of rewarding the team for feedback. Keep in mind the partnership and growing together.

❖ Persuasion and motivation

recap:

Persuasion is an essential competency of every successful leader. It is the avenue by which you lead individuals in a particular direction. Effective persuasion begins with knowing your team members and their internal motivation.

Tapping into the team members' motivation will drive team engagement. It leads to the emotional connection you will develop. The more of a connection, the higher the engagement, and ultimately, the more effective you will be at executing persuasion.

Mastering this competency begins with further developing your active listening skills and interpretation of how an individual communicates. In the next section, you will discover active listening secrets and your unique listening style.

Competency 4: Listening

Speak in a way that others love to listen.

Listen in a way that others love to speak.

—Anonymous

What does listening mean? According to the International Listening Association, listening is the attending, receiving, interpreting, and responding to messages presented aurally. Listening leverages more than just one of your senses.

Verbal communication relates to more than just the spoken word. The spoken word is only 35 percent of the intended meaning. The remaining 55 percent of communication is through body language.

On average, you listen to 450 words per minute, despite only speaking an average of 150 words per minute. You should be able to actually process everything you hear.

Wrong!

On average, you only process about 13 to 25 percent of what you hear.

Take a moment and think about that!

When is the last time you asked someone to repeat a question or heard a story and was unable to recall the details? Why?

In today's world, everything including our mind is full of distractions. These distractions are frequently on the stage of your subconscious mind hidden just to the right or left, creeping back onto center stage when least expected.

It only takes one word, sound, or smell, and instantly, you are pulled from the conversation and lost in your own thoughts. This is natural human behavior.

Effective leadership is naturally tied to listening. The more you can actively engage yourself and your mind into listening, it will result in a better understanding of your team, barriers, and processes. To better understand how to be a more active or mindful listener, you start by understanding the four types of listening styles.

People-oriented listening style demonstrates a strong focus on understanding the feelings of the individual who is speaking. This style leverages empathy and emotional intelligence to appeal to the individual's emotional side in arguments. One drawback to this style is the potential for judgment impairment.

Content-oriented listening style is more focused on the content quality of what is said. The focus is more of a fact-finding mission and credibility of the individual. This style is geared towards understanding the cause of an issue. One drawback to this style is the potential to completely discount communication if perceived to be a noncredible source.

Action-oriented listening style demonstrates more of a focus on the plan or actions of individuals. They are more concrete thinkers and focus more on getting the job done. These leaders struggle with communication about vision and large vague concepts. Some drawbacks of this style are the perception of lack of empathy towards the team and losing sight of the big picture.

Time-oriented listening style is focused on the time spent listening. These leaders are more focused on getting straight to the summary points and short answers. On average, physicians interrupt a patient within 18 seconds of speaking. This is a time-oriented listener. As a result, the patients are frustrated and many times never get to explain the main reason they are there. As a leader, you could miss valuable feedback from the team because they feel you are too busy to listen.

Can you identify with one of these styles?

The most effective listening style is a combination of two or more of these styles. Like leadership styles, with practice, you will master the most appropriate listening style. It all starts with becoming an active and mindful listener.

Mastering mindful listening is at the heart of a servant-leader. If you only listen, the individual will tell you everything you need to know to be an effective leader, just like a patient will tell the provider the diagnosis by just listening to the entire history of the patient.

Without thinking, you interact and perform activities, mindlessly becoming distracted by your subconscious stage. You have the radio on but cannot recall the names of the last songs you heard. You are driving and end up at your destination but unable to recall making the turns.

Stop. Take a deep breath. Now let's wake up that subconscious awareness.

You can practice mindful listening through the following:

1. Prepare. Clear your subconscious mind of any thoughts. This can be easily done by writing down what you feel you need to recall quickly. The need to recall a thought quickly is often the driving force about why a thought remains in your subconscious

mind.   Managing these thou
accomplished through different
school and keep a small three-b
handy. I jot down ideas to remove them
subconscious mind and ensure that I don't forget
them. Many of my colleagues manage these on apps
such as Evernote. Next, remove any physical
distractions from the area such as computers,
phones, and other electronic devices.

2. Be present. Focus on the words, the tone and
the body language. Look directly at the speaker and
focus. Avoid the temptation to mentally prepare a
rebuttal and allowing yourself to drift into your
thoughts. What is the individual saying? How is he
or she saying it?

3. Show that you are present. Convey to the
speaker that you are actively listening. Use your
nonverbal cues of head nodding, facial expressions,
and smiling. Additionally, exhibit open posturing
with open arms, uncrossed legs, and sitting up with
good posture.

4. Remove barriers while listening. Along
with removing the physical distractions, you must
continue to remove barriers throughout the
listening process by removing mental barriers.
Negative thoughts such as criticism, judgment, and
prejudice can impair your ability to listen to the
speaker actively. Also, emotions such as jealousy,
fear, denial, or apathy, can cause impairment. Be

re of your internal emotional temperature as
ou listen.

5. Respond Appropriately: Allow the speakers
to complete their full communication. Ask
clarifying questions and paraphrase what has been
said. Also, periodically recap the speaker's
comments. If the speaker's comments elicit an
emotional response, ask for clarification of the
comment. Many times, the emotional response is
due to miscommunications or misunderstandings.

Mindful listening is not achieved overnight and
takes practice. It is an essential skill for leadership
that can also can enhance your everyday life. It
provides an avenue to retain more verbal
information, increase attention span, increase self-
esteem, and thoughtful speech.

Mindful listening is the essence of a leader and
an essential quality as you pause to consider your
words and the impact of the words. The higher your
position, the more impactful your words.

❖ Listening recap:

Communication is 35 percent spoken word and
55 percent body language. Of the 35 percent, you
only process about 13 to 25 percent of what you
hear. What you process is determined by your
listening style.

Active mindful listening leverages several listening styles to ensure we are understanding the message being delivered. You must take time to prepare to listen and be 100 percent present.

The biggest benefit to mindful listening is enhancing your skill of empathy. You begin to understand the motivation behind the message. In the next chapter, you will discover the key to empathy.

Competency 5: Empathy

If you wish to know the mind of a man, listen to his words.

—Johann Wolfgang von Goethe

As leaders, one of your greatest strengths is empathy. However, allowing the emotion to make business objectives personal can be your greatest weakness. Remember not to make things personal and not to carry the weight of others' problems. Recognize that upset patients, customers, clients, and senior leaders are a result of anger at the situation or outcome. It is not reflective of how they personally feel about you.

Empathy is your ability to understand someone's feelings. Developing empathy with the ability to manage your own emotions demonstrates emotional intelligence. Developing the ability to recognize and manage emotions evolves your professional disposition.

Empathy is not a sign of weak leadership, nor

does it denote that you will give into every concern of your team. Empathy does not replace our personality. Also, it does not indicate that you will assume the personal strife or emotional baggage of an individual.

Emotional intelligence is not a reflection of one's IQ and has nothing to do with intellect. Does this mean that you can never have a bad day as a leader? Absolutely *not*! Every leader has good days and bad days.

However, it is important to consider how your disposition will impact the team. For example, if having an off day significantly impacts your mood and ability to interact with others, consider moving a team meeting. Over time, you will develop techniques that will help you with the analysis and processing of bad days to limit interruptions of your schedule.

Empathy provides the ability to develop trust with your team. The trust will provide an avenue for team to share concerns with you. Consider a team member proactively providing you information about a disgruntled individual or notification if they hear your project is missing the goal. Effective leaders take the time to understand and address individual's concerns.

Sometimes individuals just want to vent, share with you the happenings, and not expect an action. They just want the ability to share with a trusted leader. You must recognize when you need to respond. Timing is everything. Team members sharing concerns demonstrates the comfort to show their vulnerable side. This warrants the respect of your prompt attention, or you lose similar future opportunities.

Be mindful of how you interact with an individual. Leverage empathy and understand the position of each individual as it is rooted in his or her personality. The team will feel you care for them and feel respected.

Ask for the input of the individual doing the specific process before making changes that directly impact his or her daily activities. There is a high probability that they will provide you valuable feedback on how to gain efficiency. Make sure they know you have their best interest in mind and not checking up on them performing the job.

Why is empathy important in leadership? What is in it for you as a leader?

As a leader, empathy creates a sense of trust your team will develop with you, which will strengthen your leadership of the team leading to greater collaboration and engagement.

Remember, the higher team engagement leads, the higher the performance.

Some additional benefits of enhancing empathy would include:

- ❖ Ability to understand the root cause of unengaged team members or poor performers
- ❖ Ability to support struggling individuals to succeed
- ❖ Enhancement of professional relationships
- ❖ Virtual window into the team

Developing empathy begins with active listening to an individual when they speak. Listen beyond what they are saying and more about how it is said. Do you hear excitement, anger, frustration, etc.?

Next, you must put yourself in the shoes of your team. Understand their challenges and victories. What are their pain points? View initiatives from all sides, and even have a few colleagues to bounce ideas. Also encourage the team members to share how they feel about situations. Ask yourself why the individual conveys _____ (fill in the emotion) when speaking.

❖ Empathy recap:

Empathy is a vital competency of a servant-leader. You gain insights as to how an individual is subconsciously and emotionally reacting to an initiative or situation. Through empathy, you further support your relationship with the individual. You can easily identify struggling individuals and set them up for success.

You have learned the secrets to mindful listening, motivation, and persuasion. To drive your leadership strength, you act on humility. The servant leader is a humble leader. It is a leader who focuses on empathy, meeting the team's needs, and putting the team first.

Competency 6: Acting with Humility

Humility is not about thinking less of yourself; it is about thinking of yourself less.

—Anonymous

It takes a strong person to act in humility and an even stronger leader to know one's weakness. Acting with humility is the foundation of respect between the leader and the follower. It is the foundation of effective leadership.

Humility is an acknowledgement of your weaknesses. This does not require to be completed with an audience. However, you must be able to look honestly in the mirror and recognize your shortcomings. Humility makes better individuals and overall better humans in society as you shift your focus from me-driven to team-driven.

Humility is not a sign of weakness or permissiveness. It is not over or under-valuing one's worth. Humility does not equate to low self-esteem or self-defeating behavior. Lastly, it is not an avenue to self-degeneration.

Humility is the simple act of being a humble leader. It is letting go of your ego and putting others' needs before your own. It is taking the higher road and completing actions for the greater good instead for personal gain. It is a venue of effective leadership.

Without effective leadership, you will turn around and have no one to lead. Many managers begin their careers with I'm-the-boss-so-do-as-I-say mentality. Most clinical leaders start with this approach, which is understandable. It is the way you were trained as clinical professionals. You will soon learn that this autocratic style of leadership will impact your ability to lead effectively and have influential leadership.

Some leaders demonstrate lack of humility through indifference of team members' needs, indifference to feelings, irritability, and temper. These leaders often make quick, hasty judgments and speak with sharp tongues. It is rooted in pride and a sign of weak leadership. These leaders will command the following of the team. However, it is through fear. The team will never fully respect the leaders and not follow them beyond their current authority.

Humility leverages your skills of empathy to understand the needs and emotional positions of your team. It is also the ability to forgive yourself and the team in unfavorable conditions or outcomes.

Humility is one of the building blocks of servant leadership. Servant-leaders are humble and shift the focus to the team. The leader is humbled by the cause to serve or the ability to lead. It is connecting with individuals to guide them on a journey.

From every manager, there is a learning opportunity. From a bad manager, you will learn unsuccessful management techniques and sense the loss of respect that he or she encounters. Note that these management techniques that are not effective in leading the team. From a good manager, you will learn what techniques are effective. You will see ways to leverage individual's skills differently and for the betterment of the organization.

One of the greatest benefits of humility is developing the genuine trust of the team. Trust is fragile and must be held in the highest regard. The next chapter will share the secrets to gaining the team's trust even without leading in an authoritative position.

❖ Humility recap:

Acting with humility is transitioning from me-driven to team-driven leadership. It is leveraging mindful listening to put the needs of your team first and leveraging empathy to show respect for these needs.

Humility is about letting go the ego and embracing the privilege to serve as the leader of your teams. Lastly, humility is a venue for developing trust with your team.

Next, you will discover the secrets to developing trust with your team and why trust can make or break your leadership.

Competency 7: Culture of Trust

Position and authority will give you followers, but trust will make you a leader.

—Aubrey McGowan

Each person you lead is a unique individual and must be managed as such. Similar to the way you create custom treatment plans for a patient, decide on a gift to purchase for someone. People are as different as fingerprints. Each person is unique. You tailor your conversations to what motivates him or her. Consider this same approach for your team members. What motivates your team?

Effective leadership evolves from the management of relationships. Through these relationships, your team will develop trust within your leadership. You will understand the motivation or drive of your team.

There is a difference in being a leader and

holding a leadership position. People will follow your direction due to your position; however, this does not represent true leadership. Leadership is the ability to lead others because they want to follow you, not because they have to follow you. This is demonstrated by having influence over individual who you do not directly manage. People will begin following you for what you represent and not the position you hold. The win and achievement of effective leadership are demonstrated when people choose to follow you for their reasons and not for yours.

Approachability and reliability

As a leader, it is critical to be approachable. Your team members must feel they can approach you. Being approachable ensures you think before you speak. Words can be hurtful and destroy the trust you are trying so diligently to establish, especially if you are managing health care teams. Being approachable relays to your team that they can tell you anything. This will lead to the team sharing shortcomings, potential risks, and areas for your personal growth as their leader.

Leadership requires flexibility in your style and your thought processes. Like fingerprints, no two team members are alike. People are diverse in perspectives and perceptions. Be open-minded and leverage your growth mindset.

Honesty is one of the fundamentals of leadership success. Maintaining transparency and honesty are key to gaining trust. Be mindful. There will be situations that will require your full confidence of knowing your team to know what isn't appropriate to share. This can be a unique situation and should be guarded. Team members will be able to sense if you are lying.

One of the most missed opportunities is to demonstrate your honesty through admitting your mistakes. Although all leaders want to succeed, part of your job is taking risks and be willing to fail. Accepting failure and success is important. Admitting when something didn't go as planned is part of what will demonstrate honesty to the team. Demonstrating honesty and achieving trust will increase your ability to have influential leadership.

Remember stewardship. Don't play the blame game and just own mistakes.

The mistake will also provide the opportunity to managing failure. You regain credibility by creating an action plan in response to the mistake. You and the team find success in the failure.

It is vital to be fair and not play favorites. Being fair is demonstrated by providing everyone with equal opportunities. You do reserve the right to assign the opportunities to specific team members.

Ensure that those who are interested in opportunities have had a chance. Being fair ensures that you are providing the opportunities to everyone and not playing favorites.

Through opportunities, you will have superstars. Those who complete the task stretch opportunities and rise above the rest of the team. They are the individuals whom you can count on in a time of need and provide you the relief that the task will be completed to the highest level. Recognize them for their hard work.

These exceptional individuals will also need your attention and guidance. The more time you devote to team members, the more they will crave your leadership. Take the time to mentor and professionally develop the individuals. Have you spoken with them about their developmental goals?

People will rely on you as a leader to be reliable and set a good example. Arrive on time, leave when the work is done, and follow through. If you say you will do an action or task, complete it. Not following up will impact the trust you are developing with your team. Each failure to follow up will take a withdrawal out of the trust account.

Be willing to go above and beyond. Always do more than what is expected. Be willing to roll up your sleeves and do the work. You will understand the challenges your team face and the processes that work.

❖ Trust recap:

Trust must be earned from the team through one individual at a time. It is developed through fairness, objectivity, ownership, and setting others up for success.

Trust will provide you with leadership strength to influence individuals whom you directly and indirectly manage. It is also achieved through the simple act of following through.

In leadership, you give back to the individuals you lead. Through enhancing the trust competency, you provide an avenue for mentoring. You guide individuals to become better versions of themselves. In the next chapter, you will learn the best individuals to mentor and how to identify the best mentor for yourself.

Competency 8: Mentoring

The key to being a good mentor is to help people become more of who they already are—not make them more like you.

—Suze Orman

As leaders, your mission is to create other high-quality leaders. In servant leadership, you mentor others and guide them in high-quality principles. Information shared within this process is specific to the mentee's needs. As an evolving leader, find someone you want to model his or her leadership style and develop a relationship. This will be the best person for your journey. High-quality mentoring greatly enhances your chances of success.

What is mentoring?

Mentoring is a process of growth and development of two people. The mentor provides guidance or knowledge through intelligence, skills, or experience with the mentee who is the less experienced individual.

Throughout my career, I have had many mentors in my professional life. These individuals can be your personal board of directors. As a consistent influence, I have had my immediate manager, Jeff, who has fostered my development from a brand-new manager into my role today as clinical director over the largest client in our book of business. He has provided high-quality, constructive feedback and guided my path of newfound management knowledge. Whom should you consider as a mentor?

Mentors should have a genuine interest in your professional development. They should exhibit mindful listening skills and coach you on a path of solutions. The individual must retain your confidentiality and be committed to your success. Hopefully, you are having someone come to your mind. Mentoring benefits the organization, individuals, and mentors.

Skills of a mentor:

1. Open-mindedness

2. Mindful listening

3. Inquisitive

4. Honesty

5. Self-awareness

For the organization, there are many benefits. These include knowledge transfer, structured learning, identifying of high potential individuals, fostering an organizational culture, and fine-tuning soft skills.

For the mentor, the benefits include building relationships, supporting and driving innovation, increasing professional contacts, enhancement of coaching skills, and personal satisfaction.

For the identified mentee or mentored individual, benefits include developing a new skill of guiding others. They gain professional growth, in-depth understanding of the organization and culture, and the potential to mentor in the future.

Is reverse mentoring the future of leadership development?

The millennial generation has generated disruptive innovation throughout every organization known today. Millennials have brought technology, new expertise, and new viewpoints to the corporate table. Without innovation, the organization would fail.

Reverse mentoring is a new process of flipping the top-down learning into mentoring senior level executives by junior team members. Companies are discovering new innovative ways of leveraging social media and technology. This style of mentoring bridges the gaps between both individuals. These senior mentors learn about new technology and culture. The junior mentor has a role model and career coach.

The reverse mentoring relationship has become pivotal at cultural insensitivities. It has strengthened both generations of collaborative partnerships and advancing organizations.

❖ Mentoring recap:

Mentoring is a way of giving back and passing on all the skills you have learned through your journey. It is also a mechanism by which you can become mentees and better understand new skills, technology, and generational cultural differences.

You demonstrate genuine interest and commitment to the individuals we lead and mentor. Provide constructive feedback and remain open-minded, honest, and inquisitive throughout your guidance.

In the next section, you will examine the role of the coach. While a mentor guides an individual through the mentor's previous experience and knowledge, a coach guides someone on a path leveraging the individual's knowledge and experience to define actions to achieve a goal or solve a problem.

Competency 9: Coaching

Leaders help those who are doing poorly do better and those who are doing well do great.

—Anonymous

When is it necessary to use coaching? How to you know when to coach? Coaching is designed for behavioral changes. Consider behavioral changes as modifiable risk factors for a heart disease patient—aspects of the individual that is within his power to change.

There are situations in organizations when it becomes necessary to introduce coaching. Typically, performance and skills enhancements are the primary reasons a manager would coach an individual. This is a type of coaching that focuses on core skills that are required to carry out tasks and handle work responsibilities effectively. Skills coaching is targeted at improving the basic skills of an individual for the general well-being and growth of the company or establishment.

Some additional situations would include:

- **Change-management** coaching is implemented before a major change in the structure or work pattern within an organization. This helps to align the attitude and behavior of the individual with the new work structure and condition to optimize output. This would help everyone involved to adjust to the new changes and mentally process the changes.

  Think back to when you had a concern about changes in leadership such as a manager. The same concern or anxiety will happen to your team. Consider change as an opportunity for growth and convey this to the team. This is also an opportunity for you to lead through any disruption of your processes.

- **Career coaching** focuses on coaching the individual's career interests. Career coaching assesses the individual's career capabilities and helps him to adjust and improve his career output. It brings about a personal reevaluation of career outlook and development plan where the individual being coached emerges with more clarity in career awareness. This coaching helps the employee adapt to the change in his or her given role or work position within the organization.

- **Personal life coaching** focuses on people who are being coached on a very personal level. It explores their aspirations, needs, wishes, all they want to make of themselves, and all they need to make out of life. Personal or life coaching provides support for them to make changes that reposition them in life.

- **Team facilitation coaching** is with the purpose of enhancing output for a particular goal of an organization. Team facilitation extensively improves self-confidence and the performance of a team in laying down strategies and execution of tasks.

In the clinical setting, this would be providing strategic direction to the care team. For example, 30 percent of the diabetic patients are not in control of their diabetes. The new focus is driving better glucose control in this population. Coaching would include discussing with the team on how to achieve diabetic disease management control.

- **Shortage of talents**: When an organization runs into the dilemma of a shortage of team members in manning special positions, it would be a cheaper and more cost-effective approach to coach the current team. This intervention would develop their skills and make them capable of manning whatever position is available.

Now that you have identified when to coach, let's focus on the fundamentals of coaching.

In today's workplace environment, coaching has dominated as the most effective means of engagement. Coaching is an ongoing interactive process that leads individuals to discover insights, take ownership, and develop actionable goals on performance and development. Engagement through insights leads to sustainable change. The individual isn't broken or of less intelligence. Many times, individuals become obsessed with the presenting problem and lose sight of the lesson.

Coaching is designed as a mechanism for learning lessons from past experiences and creating self-discovery to modify future outcomes. Understanding when coaching would not be effective is important for every leader. Mental illness, legal policy violations (harassment), family-dynamic changes, and state of emergency crisis are better left to professionals and consultation of your human resources representative (HBR Guide to Coaching Employees, 2015). It is also critical not to turn a coaching session into a blame game or gripe session.

Setting the scene

Coaching is essential to developing a growth mindset, which is vital to the succession of you and your team.

Any coaching session requires preparation! Be open-minded and a mindful listener. Keep in mind a 4:1 ratio of listening to speaking. Any more than that, you are teaching and not coaching. Good coaches know their own biases and how the individual fits into the big picture. A *great* coach will develop while guiding to the company's missions and goals.

While coaching, be mindful of your presence, and keep the acronym STOP in mind:

- Slow speech

- Tone of voice: lower-than-normal speaking voice

- Open questions and posture

- <u>P</u>ause for active listening and eye contact

Creating a thriving environment will instill confidence, thus leading to positive changes in performance. Also, for effective coaching, you must have a connection with the individual. Caution yourself not to fix the problem. Keep in mind that your team member is not broken.

How do you know when to coach? Coaching is designed for behavioral changes. Think of these as modifiable risk factors or things that we have the power to change. Aspects of the individual that is within his or her power to change would include weight, diet, exercise, response to a situation, etc.

A quick coaching method is leveraging the GROW model. The GROW model was developed by Sir John Whitmore and Graham Alexander in 1980s and has several variations.

Let's look at each component of the GROW method to understand the implications:

Goals

For coaching, determine the long- and short-term goals. The long-term goal is the behavior desired to be changed. The short-term goals are goals for each coaching session. Remember that this coaching process will require more than one session.

Before coaching an individual, consider the goal of the coaching session. What would be the successful outcomes? What behavior do you want to see modified?

Consider your management goals surrounding what behavior you want to modify. Is it a modifiable behavior or an innate personality characteristic? Personality characteristics are not modifiable. However, these elements are the opportunity to facilitate the individual's understanding of how others perceive their traits.

For example, have you encountered an individual who says, "I know I am/can be___ (fill in the blank)"? While this is an innate characteristic, the individual recognizes that it can be a challenge for others.

Now, consider reasonable goals for the coachee. Their insights should lead them to a personal goal that achieves the manager's long-term goal.

When setting goals, make them **SMART**:

S=Specific: what would you like to achieve?

M=Measurable: how will you know you are successful?

A=Achievable: what steps will you take?

R=Relevant: can you describe your perfect world?

T=Time-bound: when do you see yourself reaching your goal?

Consider the goals, make them SMART, and write them down.

Reality

You will ask open-ended questions that lead to describing the situation objectively. Consider the most common and use the coachee's words to the questions:

What do you mean by_____?

Anything else?

Could you tell me more about_____?

Leveraging one of these three top questions will provide an open avenue for conversations, eliminate your personal bias, and avoid possible interjecting self-proposed conclusions of the situation. Practice the questions in role play with a colleague. Say each question more slowly than your regular tone and in a slightly deeper tone. Notice how the person responds. This will create a calming environment and provide a more comfortable and defused atmosphere to discuss the situation.

Ensure that you are leveraging your active listening skills to focus on what and how the situation is being described. The team member will tell you everything you need to know if you just listen. Continue with the discussion until the individual has insight.

Options

The options step is devised to elicit insights specific to solutions for the problem. Think of this as the brainstorming session. Have the individual leverage personal insights to guide themselves towards a solution. What are their thoughts about solving the problem? While your goal is eliciting insights, some individuals may need a suggestion to start the process as this will probably be awkward for them during the first session.

Consider these questions to elicit insight:

What could have been done differently?

What if you did nothing?

What obstacles are in your way?

What is your first step?

Will

In the will stage, you will guide in the choice of one of the options and create an action plan similar to a treatment or care plan for a patient. You will need to assess the motivation of the team member.

Consider these questions to guide the conversation:

Which options work best for you?

How will you start?

What obstacles will you encounter?

How will you overcome the obstacles?

When shall we meet again to check your progress?

As the plan emerges, write it down. Ask the individuals how they will hold themselves accountable as well as the preferred frequency you hold them accountable.

After the coaching session, provide follow-up support. This will be a new process for them and when they need you most. This is where they will test the options and will of the GROW model. There will be obstacles and possible confusion. This is another opportunity for coaching. If you always provide the answer, folks will always line up at your door needing an answer.

❖ Coaching recap:

Coaching is used to help an individual discover solutions through leveraging their insights. Coaching is a standard tool used today and designed to learn lessons from the past to create self-discovery for the future.

Coaching requires preparation and leveraging tools. Tools such as the GROW model will provide a systematic avenue for guidance.

To be an effective coach, you must develop your personal competency of foresight. Cultivating foresight provides you with the ability to learn from your own past. Next, you will explore cultivating foresight, a quick four-step method to problem solving, and making high-quality decisions every time.

Competency 10: Foresight

By failing to prepare, you are preparing to fail.

—Benjamin Franklin

Foresight is a unique skill of the servant leader used to guide their decisions through learning from the past, mindfulness of the present, and understanding the potential consequences of the future. Through the diversity of the team you create, you surround yourselves with individuals who offer different perspectives of a situation. They provide a fresh view into your everyday decisions. Foresight provides a venue for making intuitive and educated decisions.

There are several ways to cultivate foresight:

1. **Lead with diversity.** This relates back to self-awareness. When you surround yourselves with diverse individuals, you develop a more well-rounded team. By only surrounding ourselves with like-minded individuals, your teams will have

your strengths and our weaknesses.

2. **Active mindful listening.** Listening is a critical skill of any leader, especially a servant-leader. Are you hearing similar concerns from several team members? If so, by foresight, you could determine an emerging trend or future consequence.

3. **Read widely**. Develop an industry understanding. You are not expected to be subject matter expert in your field. However, you are expected to have a general understanding of the industry. This is vital to understanding how to best lead within the industry.

4. **Systematic** approach. Think systematically. Consider the situation and leverage your foresight to determine the consequence of decisions.

5. **Predictions**. Practice making predicttions alone as well as with your team. Test the predictions against reality. Are you identifying trends?

One of the vital skills of leveraging foresight is problem solving.

Problem Solving

Problem solving is fundamental to every leader's role. Problems are truly opportunities to develop more efficiencies, grow the business, or discover innovation. You may be the one solving the problem or supporting those who do. Confidence will convey to the team your ability to think systemically on how to best tackle this new endeavor. Solving problems are done systemically.

Four SIMPLE steps to Problem Solving

1. Defining the problem or opportunity

2. Outlining possible solutions

3. Evaluation of each solution

4. Implementation of a solution

In step one, you define the problem. Leveraging a tool such as the Five Whys is a quick method to determine the root cause. The Five Whys were developed through the Toyota production system and have become the industry standard for identification of underlying stimulus of the problem. When a problem arises, you simply ask why five times. At the fifth why, you will discover the true root of the problem. Here's an example of the Five Whys:

PROBLEM: The specialist is rescheduling the patient's appointments when scheduled at the primary care clinic.

- **WHY?** The referring provider's notes are not at the specialist's office before the appointment.

- **WHY?** The notes are not being faxed promptly before the appointment.

- **WHY?** The notes are incomplete.

- **WHY?** The providers do not have the designated charting time on the schedule.

- **WHY?** The providers' schedules have not been updated.

As you can see, this is a valuable tool that provides a way of peeling back the layers of the problem and discovering the true issue. Once the providers' schedules were updated to have designated charting time, the patients were seen at the originally scheduled appointment time.

In step two, you develop solutions to the problem. Consider this as brainstorming to solve the problem. In an ideal world, everyone would be able to sit together and generate creative solutions. In many environments, you have blocking that leads to only a few boisterous individuals providing input, while others shy away. Many shy individuals lack the confidence to share, feel their ideas are silly, or fear teasing from the group. One quick alternative is having the group write down the solution without their names. Then the solutions are read aloud for the team to analyze.

In step three, you analyze the difficult solutions through decision making. Decision making involves determining the credibility of the source, determining effects the decision, cost-benefit analysis, and ethical consideration. After vetting the solutions and identifications of single best solution that should be implemented, consider plan B.

In step four, you implement the identified solution. Thoughtful planning will maximize success at solving the problem and minimize the risk. Depending on the solution, implementation could be a simple process change or a full project plan. Utilize your resources wisely.

There is no guarantee that every decision you make as leaders will be a successful one. Your goal is to have tools in our toolbox to make high-quality decisions and troubleshoot through your problem-solving skills.

Decision quality

Leaders make decisions every day, and the continued enhancement of this skill needs nurturing daily. Not all leaders are created equally and able to make a sound decision. Decisions will either make or break a leader. Many times, failure as a leader is related to a single bad decision. It is often related to multiple poor decisions compounded on each other.

Although it is important to remember, even good leaders make bad decisions. A poor decision does not dictate you as a bad leader. Your leadership maturity will determine your management of the effects of a bad decision. It is important to always own your mistake and not place blame with another individual.

*How do you **avoid** making poor decisions?*

In making quality decisions, you will need to understand how to categorize the overwhelming amount of information you will receive. You will receive information from many points of interest. However, keep in mind that not all points are equal. One of the first issues to consider when processing information is the source.

Information is filtered based on the source. Is the source credible or biased? Consider the motivation of the source. Why are they sharing the information? Is it a vested interest in the outcome of the decision, to show another's shortcomings, or for their personal gain?

Also integrate a framework into your decision-making strategy, and standardize the process with each decision to ensure that your decisions are of the highest quality. It will not guarantee a perfect decision each time. However, it will lessen the chances of having a bad decision.

Five steps to high-quality decisions:

1. **Situation analysis**: current versus future state. Who are the stakeholders? What is the impact of the decision? What are the direct and indirect effects? Do you have the information needed to make an unbiased decision?

2. **Effects of the decision.** Every decision made will become public. If the decision was made visible to every person you encounter, how would you feel? What would the stakeholders think of your decision? No decision is made in a box, and the impact of every decision will be on the team and/or process.

3. **Moral compass.** Every decision should be guided by your moral compass and your integrity. If you feel the need to hide a decision, chances are it is a bad decision. Decisions should be made and you should stand tall with confidence.

4. **Cost-benefit analysis.** Do the benefits of the decision outweigh the cost and risk of the decision? What if the cost is more than expected?

5. **Plan B**. Always have a backup plan. What is the strategy if your decision creates barriers? What if you are unable to meet the expectations of others or of your key stakeholders? A well-prepared plan has an equally viable backup plan.

Strategic decision making involves the long-term decisions made to create an organization's mission, goals, objectives, and values. The steps outlined above will also facilitate decisions made regarding the strategy of the organization.

❖ Foresight recap:

Foresight is the ability to leverage previous experiences or decisions to guide present or future decisions. You cultivate foresight in being open-minded to the diverse views of the team.

Decision making should be simple yet able to leverage systematic methodology to ensure that the highest quality decisions are made. A poor outcome reflects a poor decision and not necessarily a poor leader. Exercise consistency on the five quality decision steps, and leverage the problem-solving tool to guide decisions.

Foresight is also used to guide you towards the best approach to communicate your vision and the vision of the organization. You will know the motivation and benefits of the team. In the next chapter, you will discover how to attract high-performing team members who will be committed to your leadership vision.

Competency 11: Vision

Leadership is the capacity to translate vision into reality.

—*Warren G. Bennis*

Vision is timeless and represents the overall values, beliefs, and goals of an organization or leader. Over time, the strategies will evolve and change; however, the vision is unwavering. Vision is the purpose and what matters most.

It is easy to get caught up in the everyday battles. Don't lose sight of the war. What is the vision of the team? What is the mission? Complete actions surrounding the end goal. Ask yourself if this initiative is moving towards your goal. If not, refocus.

What is the strength of vision?

Strong vision conveyed through an effective leader is evidence of conviction. It demonstrates to the rest of the team the belief in the vision and resonates through the strategies.

These strong leaders will draw in followers who also believe in the vision conveyed. The result is a high-performing team dedicated to achieving the vision at any cost.

As an effective leader, you must enhance our skills of communication. To convey your conviction in the vision, you must be able to communicate it clearly. Communication begins with citing the vision in a clear and simple manner. Make the vision something everyone can easily understand.

Consider the impact of these vision statements:

Apple: To design the best personal computer in the world.

Life is Good: Spreading power of optimism.

Nordstrom: To give customers the most compelling shopping experience.

JetBlue: To inspire humanity—both in the air and on the ground.

You must communicate the vision as well as clear direction and action plans. Generally, this is easy to achieve as new team members move into the mix. The leadership opportunity lies in leading the current team members into the vision.

How to lead current team member success

Change is a scary word for many individuals. It represents uncertainty and ambiguity. This fear can be calmed by your approach to change. Replace the negative connotation of change with the more positive spin of opportunity. Shift to a leader's growth mindset.

What is change? Change is the opportunity for evolution. As you become more comfortable with evolution, so will your team. The team will look to you on how to respond to change. As in all facets, you are on stage and the team is watching your response—both verbal and nonverbal cues.

It is important to keep in mind that evolution is critical to the sustainable growth of a company. Without evolution, organizations will stay at status quo, fail to deliver new products to the industry, and ultimately fail to thrive. AT&T is a great example of a modern day of evolution.

Consider the smartphone and how integrated this small piece of hardware is into your culture. The Bell Telephone Company began telephonic services through manually connecting customers through switchboard operators. Over time, the operator model could not be sustained due to the volume of customers. The model became automated and the household dial phone evolved.

r was empowered to contact any
out the middle person.

...d evolved, so did the Bell Company.
...1 1983, AT&T purchased the Bell Company. This lead to the expansion of cellular technology allowing customer to call individuals while on the go. Looking around today, it's hard to imagine life without your smartphones and apps. Had the Bell Company resisted the evolution of the industry, you would now have a different landscape in the cellular industry without AT&T.

Throughout history, there are numerous examples of leaders managing a team through strategic initiatives, transitions of leadership, acquisitions, or even changes in the vision of companies.

As a leader or a coach, you are responsible for moving the team into different directions or evolution as a change agent. To be an effective change agent, you must exhibit influence over an organization, which is achieved through the multidimensional aspect of trust.

So how do you evolve or change a team?

The most effective model was developed by Dale Carnegie by envisioning the future state and how you will lead your team to achieve the future state.

Consider the *present* state:

1. Establish the motivation for change

2. Analyze the situation

3. Plan the direction

Now consider the *future* state:

1. Implement the change

2. Review and assess the impact of the change

3. Modify and adjust as needed

You now have a detailed plan on how to deal with change. Take each step and dive deep into the information driving the step. You will have a good understanding of the change, the impact, and how to ensure success with your team. With these simple steps, you can lead your team through evolution with confidence.

❖ Vision recap:

Vision demonstrates the values, beliefs, and goals of an organization. Vision is timeless and unshaken by changes in strategy. Strong vision conveyed by the leader will attract strong like-minded followers.

Vision statements should be simple and repeatable by leaders as well as the team. Change management principles are useful in guiding resistant team members into the vision.

Interpersonal skills such as communication and change management are enhanced through the continuous development of every leader. Leaders must continue to learn and grow as professionals to facilitate their continued success. In the next section, you will learn how to be a steward of your own personal leadership journey and know where to focus on your path.

Competency 12: Continuous Development

The way of success is the way of continuous pursuit of knowledge.

—Napoleon Hill

Leadership is a self-guided journey that requires continuous learning and professional growth. Continuous improvement is striving to improve the status quo and impacts all areas of leadership. Every day in your role, you strive to improve the experience for your team, your customers or patients, your internal or external matrix partners, your products, your patient care delivery, etc.

While you cannot change the world overnight, it's the small changes over time that make the biggest impact and lead to your legacy. View each day and situation as an opportunity. Strive to leave situations better than you found them.

Making large shifts to significant improvement

doesn't happen overnight. This modality requires planning and change-management principles. Ultimately, if you are focused on making large changes quickly, then you must adapt and condition the team, and ensure that you have quality checks in place. This is a separate process and mindset. If this is your goal, reference the change-management section.

Throughout any business, quality control and continuous improvement are vital to the sustainability. Quality control ensures that the products are generated to yield a consistent level of quality at status quo or improved. Additionally, there is a reduced risk of mistakes. Within the clinical environment, safety-syringe engagement would be an example where you would expect continuous quality. With safety syringes, you expect any syringe to properly deploy the safety feature of the syringe to prevent unwarranted sticks. Another consideration is the level of care delivered by a health care professional. For example, when someone sustains an injury to the arm and has deformity, you expect an X-ray of the arm to be completed.

Continuous improvement is an ongoing process geared towards improving products and or services. These improvements could be small to drive efficiency or reduce nonvalue-added steps. These improvements could also be significant, leading to a complete revamping of an entire process. For example, one clinic wanted to target reduction of collections. A simple change in the office procedure of collecting funds from the patient while the patient was in the clinic dramatically reduced the collection volume.

There are many tools available through lean health care and Six Sigma. Take a moment to learn about these principles.

For now, let's look closely at the continuous improvement from a leadership view. You desire to learn and grow is what will ultimately distinguish you from your followers. As you take the role of leader, understand that it is a continuous journey and not a destination. Your leadership will continue to grow over time. Your role is to nurture the path.

No one will do this for you! We must be stewards of our own professional development. How do you know your weakness? Many resources can provide insight into your area of professional growth opportunities. There are several assessments that can be completed, such as strength-based, 360 reviews, and so on. One of my personal favorites is based upon Steve Arneson's book, *Bootstrap Leadership*.

Arneson provides a simple quiz at the beginning of the book that provides insight into your leadership strengths and weaknesses. The first section is based on how the world views your leadership and how to elicit feedback on your style. The second section focuses on your leadership toolbox and developing new skills. The third section focuses on expanding your horizon and exploring inspiration, innovation, and diversity. The fourth section speaks to stepping outside your comfort zone as it is only through discomfort that you grow and develop. The last section guides on how to have long-term followers and continue to develop your leadership (Arneson, 2010).

As I stated before, leadership is a journey, not a destination. Some individuals are born with an innate ability to lead. However, even those individuals must continue to grow. There are several stages of development along this leadership journey according to John C. Maxwell in *The 21 Irrefutable Laws of Leadership* (Maxwell, 2007).

According to Maxwell, there are really four phases as defined below:

1. **I Don't Know What I Don't Know:** this phase is the ineffective and unaware stage.

2. **I Know What I Don't Know:** this phase is the ineffective but aware stage.

3. **I Know and Grow, and It Starts to Show:** this phase is the effective and

aware stage.

4. **I Simply Go Because of What I Know:** this phase is the effective and unaware stage.

There are no Lone Ranger leaders. If you are alone, then you are leading no one. The greatest impact is what you do over time to strengthen your skills and competencies.

❖ Continuous development recap:

As with many professions, continuous development is vital to sustaining success, and leadership is no different. Continuous learning involves learning new skills and techniques of leadership. It is also important to stay current on any changes within your industry or professional field.

There are many resources available to facilitate your growth and identify areas of your leadership weakness. Tools such as 360 assessments and strength-based questionnaires are a couple of examples. Be open-minded and honest with yourself along your leadership journey.

Conclusion

*The servant-leader is servant first. It begins with
the natural feeling that one wants to serve. Then
conscious choice brings one to aspire to lead.*

—Robert Greenleaf

Servant leadership is a timeless concept describing individuals who lead by serving others and placing their needs above their own. The leader empowers individuals, focuses on growth, and ensures that their basic needs are met. Guided by an internal moral compass, the servant-leader leads with the highest integrity and moral.

There are 12 core competencies leveraged in servant leadership:

- **Self-awareness** is the ability to represent and know your true self, openness to suggestion, and knowing the impact of your emotions on the team.

- **Stewardship** is accepting responsibility and accountability for your own actions as well as the team's actions.

- **Persuasion** is the avenue by which you lead individuals, which is guided by knowing the individuals and their internal *motivations*.

- **Active listening** is actively engaging in the language that is verbally and nonverbally communicated.

- **Empathy** is understanding how an individual is subconsciously and emotionally reaction to an individual or situation.

- **Acting with humility** is being a humble leader, showing leadership as a privilege, and transition from me-driven to team-driven leadership.

- **Culture of trust** is created by one individual at a time through fairness, objectivity, ownership, and setting others up for success.

- **Mentoring** is a process of growth and development to guide an individual through into more of who they already are.

- **Coaching** is leveraging the growth mindset of an individual to guide him or her on self-discovery of solutions or

achieving personal goals.

- **Foresight** is used to guide the leader through learning from the past, mindfulness of the present, and understanding the potential consequences of the future.

- **Vision** demonstrates the values, beliefs and goals of the organization or leaders, which will be unwavering with the evolution of strategies.

- **Continuous development** is a self-guided journey that evokes continuous learning and growth to improve and sustain your leadership success.

Leveraging each of these core competencies will ensure you are leading to the highest integrity and your true self. You will experience a more self-fulling role with team-based instead of me-based management and gain the unwavering respect of your team.

Thank you for purchasing this book!

I hope the book has provided you insights into your leadership style and management. Each one of us is different and unique in the approach to leadership.

Never give up and know you are strong. Lead with your empathetic strength and be guided by your moral compass.

Reviews are *critical* to the survival of any indie author like me! If you have benefited from this book or feel someone else would, please take a few moments and rate this book!

Sharing is caring!

MORE FREE STUFF!

Are you interested in **FREE** leadership books? Sign up to be on the launch team!

You get an advanced **FREE** reviewer copy of my next book. You would need to read the book within a week, provide feedback, and leave a review on Go Live day! ☺

It's that **EASY**! To join, check out my facebook page: www.facebook.com/carabramlett/

I would love to hear from you! Share your journey or challenge you are experiencing. Email me at carabramlett@yahoo.com.

Enjoy the journey!

Cara Bramlett

P.S. Don't forget your bonus gifts!

www.facebook.com/carabramlett/

References

Arneson, S. (2010). Bootstrap Leadership. In S. Arneson. San Francisco: Berrett-Koehler Publishers, Inc.

Gallo, A. (2017). *HBR Guide to Dealing with Conflict*. Boston: Harvard Business Review Press.

HBR Guide to Coaching Employees. (2015). Boston: Harvard Business Review Press.

Maxwell, J. C. (2007). The 21 Irrefutable Laws of Leadership. In J. C. Maxwell, *The 21 Irrefutable Laws of Leadership*. Dallas: Thomas Nelson.

Riggio, P., & E., R. (2011, August 22). *10 Rules for High Performing Teams*. Retrieved from Psychology Today: https://www.psychologytoday.com/blog/cutting-edge-leadership/201108/10-rules-high-performing-teams

Check out these other books!

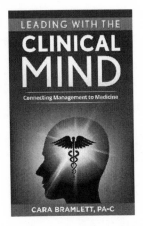

LEADING WITH THE CLINICAL MIND: Connecting Management to Medicine

Imagine leading your high-functioning team to meet the organization's goals as an industry leader. You are followed for who you are and what you represent. Your team members willingly share adversity and pending threats. Make this a reality through understanding leadership techniques through our clinical mindset. Learn how to relate to each member of your team and know how to maximize each one's unique skills. Learn how to leverage skills of communication, coaching, conflict resolution, and much more!

As clinical professionals, you have naturally dedicated your life to serving patients. Understanding how to relate leadership to medicine makes the transition smooth for clinically minded individuals.

Any clinical professional can be an effective leader! This book will teach you management concepts through medical analogies.

You will also discover the following:

•Ten techniques to combat feeling overwhelmed

•Activities to develop emotional intelligence

•The most successful method of employee engagement

•How to speak so others love to listen

•Steps to a call-to-action plan

•Tips for managing high-volume emails

•And much more!

About the Author

Cara Bramlett, PA-C is a clinical program director for a large health care organization. She continues to practice weekly in a primary care setting. Cara is passionate about ensuring each leader recognizes his or her dream of achieving leadership.

Through the promotion of self-improvement and professional development, Cara inspires and motivates others to deliver excellence in patient care and leadership leveraging integrity, honesty, collaboration, and empathy. Cara supports individuals and organizations through strong technical skills, problem solving, innovation, and unique clinical strategic perspective vested in evidence-based clinical practice.

Cara enjoys spending time with her five kids and two grandkids. She also enjoys spending time with her husband, riding motorcycles, and playing golf.

Follow me on Amazon or connect with me on LinkedIn.

Made in the USA
Middletown, DE
07 April 2019